T2-BQE-809

Riggs, Kate.
Samurai /

2011. WITHDRAWN
33305224006316
mh   10/07/11

GREAT WARRIORS

SAMURAI

KATE RIGGS

CREATIVE C EDUCATION

Published by Creative Education
P.O. Box 227, Mankato, Minnesota 56002
Creative Education is an imprint of The Creative Company
www.thecreativecompany.us

Design and production by Stephanie Blumenthal
Art direction by Rita Marshall
Printed by Corporate Graphics in the United States of America

Photographs by Alamy (J Marshall-Tribaleye Images, Mary Evans Picture Library, Popperfoto), Corbis
(Alinari Archives, Asian Art & Archaeology, Inc., Bettman,
Werner Forman, Michael Maslan Historic Photographs), iStockphoto

Copyright © 2011 Creative Education
International copyright reserved in all countries. No part of this book may be reproduced
in any form without written permission from the publisher.

Library of Congress Cataloging-in-Publication Data
Riggs, Kate.
Samurai / by Kate Riggs.
p. cm. — (Great warriors)
Summary: A simple introduction to the Japanese warriors known as samurai, including their
history, lifestyle, weapons, and how they remain a part of today's culture through the martial arts.
Includes index.
ISBN 978-1-60818-003-5
1. Samurai—Japan—History—Juvenile literature I. Title. II. Series.
DS827.S3R54 2011
952—dc22   2009048810
CPSIA: 040110   PO1137
First Edition
2 4 6 8 9 7 5 3 1

TABLE OF CONTENTS

Sometimes people fight.
They fight for food. They fight for land.
Or sometimes they fight for sport.
Samurai were warriors who fought
other people to protect their **master**
and his land.

Samurai spent their lives keeping others safe

Samurai warriors lived in Japan. They began fighting almost 900 years ago. A warrior came from a family of samurai. Every samurai helped defend his master. The master was called a daimyo (*DIE-myoh*).

Samurai sometimes fought on battlefields

THE YAMATO (*YAH-MAH-TOH*) PEOPLE WERE FIGHTERS IN JAPAN BEFORE THE SAMURAI.

CHILDREN IN JAPAN PRACTICE THE MARTIAL ART OF
KENDO. THEY FIGHT WITH STICKS, NOT SWORDS.

Boys started training when they were about seven. A boy's teacher was an older samurai. Young samurai learned how to read and write. They studied **martial arts**. Then they learned how to use weapons.

Many young people in Japan still learn martial arts

Weapons were important to samurai. The warriors thought that their swords were like parts of their own bodies. A samurai sword was long and curved. It was called a katana (*kuh-TAH-nuh*).

Only one side of the katana was sharp

SOME SAMURAI USED BOWS AND ARROWS ON THE
BATTLEFIELD. THEY COULD SHOOT FROM FAR AWAY.

Some samurai carried a spear. Others used a metal folding fan. It could cut people like a knife. A suit of **armor** protected the samurai in battle. Plates of metal covered each arm and leg. Another plate covered the chest.

Samurai wore wide, metal helmets on their heads

A SAMURAI'S SUIT OF ARMOR
WAS LIKE WHAT KNIGHTS
WORE, BUT IT DID NOT WEIGH
AS MUCH.

A warrior fought to the death. Samurai were not afraid to die for their master. If samurai lost a battle, they felt like they had let their master down. So some samurai killed themselves as **punishment**.

Samurai would rather die than fail their master

Samurai did not fight all the time. They were quiet and peaceful when they were not fighting. Samurai respected other people. They were loyal. And they were **self-disciplined**.

Samurai wore their hair in what is called a topknot

SAMURAI WORE LONG, FLOW-
ING ROBES CALLED KIMONOS
(*KIH-MOH-NOHZ*)
UNDER THEIR ARMOR.

A man named Oda Nobunaga (*OH-dah noh-boo-NAH-gah*) was a famous samurai in the 1500s. He wanted to rule the entire country of Japan. One of the last samurai was Saigo Takamori (*SY-goh tah-kah-MOH-ree*). He lived in the 1800s.

Saigo Takamori wore a uniform instead of a kimono

By the 1800s, Japan did not need samurai anymore. The country had a big army that protected everyone, not just masters. Today, people use the skills of the samurai in martial arts. Samurai live on in them!

Japanese leaders in the late 1800s fought against samurai

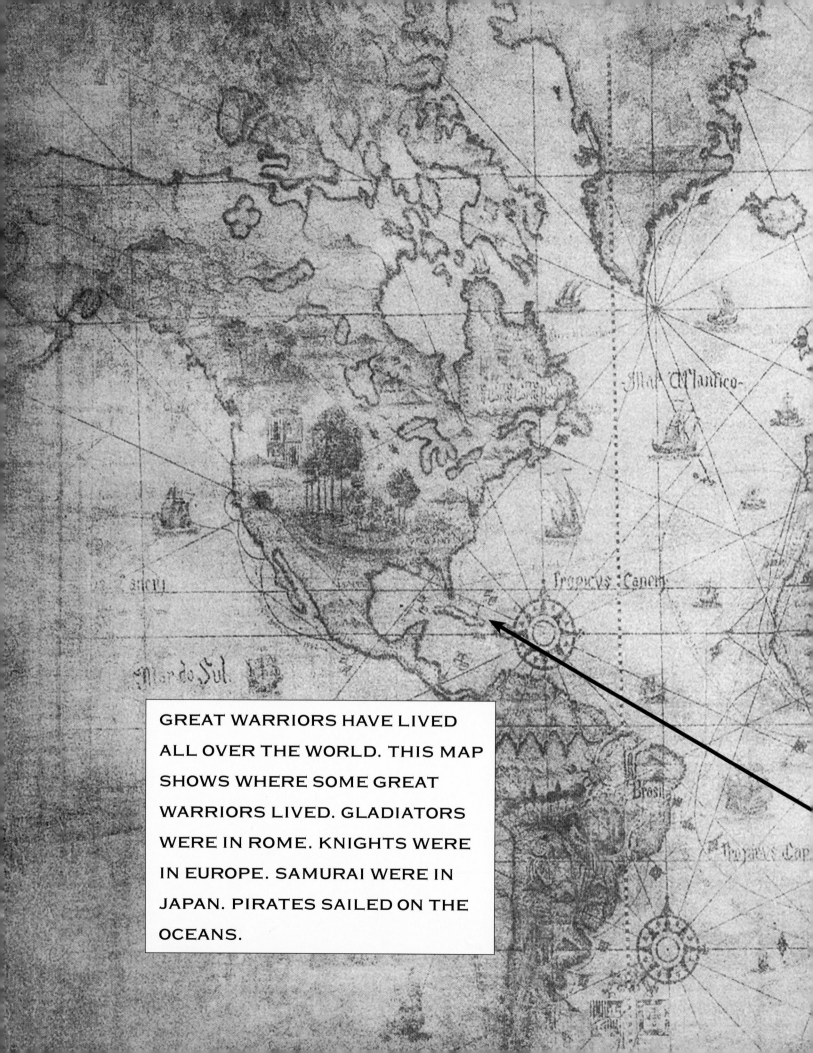

GREAT WARRIORS HAVE LIVED ALL OVER THE WORLD. THIS MAP SHOWS WHERE SOME GREAT WARRIORS LIVED. GLADIATORS WERE IN ROME. KNIGHTS WERE IN EUROPE. SAMURAI WERE IN JAPAN. PIRATES SAILED ON THE OCEANS.

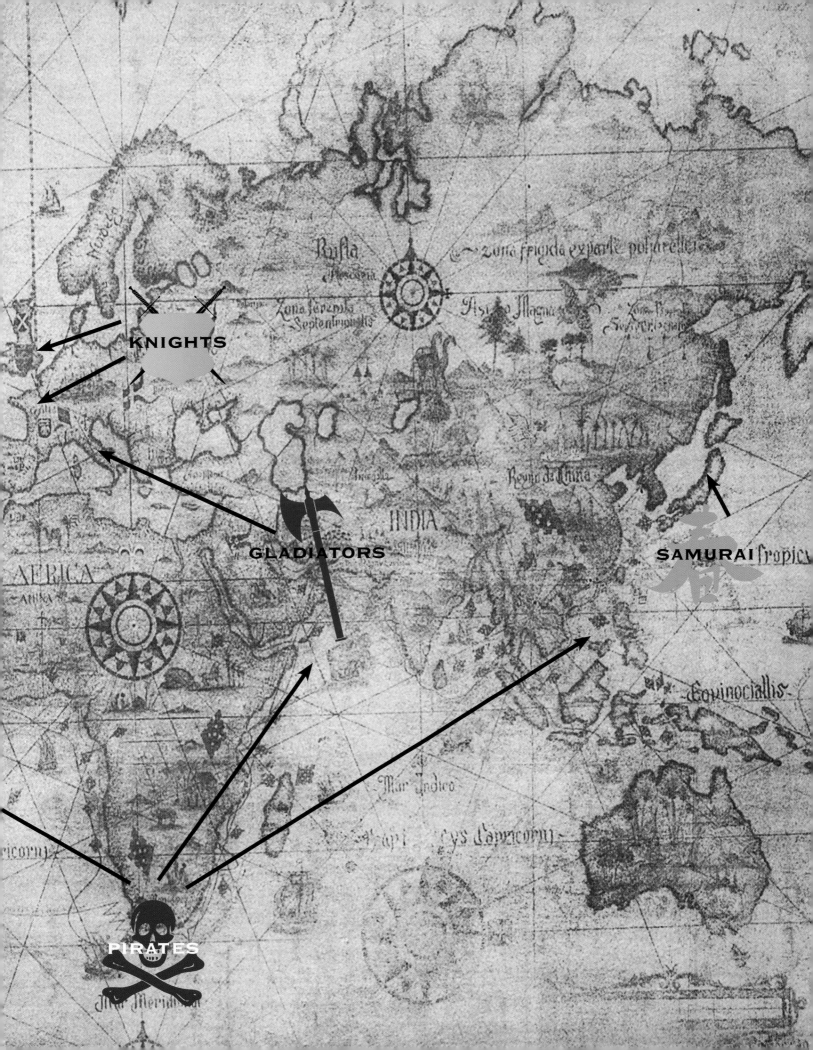

GLOSSARY

armor—metal coverings that samurai wore to protect their bodies in battle

martial arts—sports or skills that people learn to defend themselves in a fight

master—a powerful man who has people working for him

punishment—the action taken for breaking a rule or doing something wrong

self-disciplined—having control over your own feelings and actions

READ MORE

MacDonald, Fiona. *How to Be a Samurai Warrior.* Washington, D.C.: National Geographic Children's Books, 2007.

Ollhoff, Jim. *Samurai.* Edina, Minn.: ABDO Publishing, 2008.

INDEX